HEAVEN'S HEROES
The Sneaky Serpent

Kristin Lehr

Illustrated by Alicia Berry

ELK LAKE PUBLISHING INC

PUBLISHING THE POSITIVE
Plymouth, Massachusetts

Cover and Interior Design: Derinda Babcock

Editor(s): Derinda Babcock, Deb Haggerty

Illustrated by: Alicia Berry
Author Represented by WordWise Media Services

Library Cataloging Data

Names: Lehr, Kristin (Kristin Lehr)

The Sneaky Serpent / Kristin Lehr

38 p. 21.6 cm × 21.6 cm (8.5 in. × 8.5 in.)

Identifiers: ISBN-13: 978-1-64949-299-9 (paperback) | 978-1-64949-300-2 (trade hardcover) | 978-1-64949-301-9 (trade paperback) | 978-1-64949-302-6 (ebook)

Key Words: Children ages 4 to 8, Picture book, Christian, Bible story, Spiral learning, Read together book, Adam and Eve

Library of Congress Control Number: 2021941481 Nonfiction

This is Adam and Eve.

Thank you, God, for loving me. I will follow you.

A garden that's home to Adam and Eve.

Thank you, God, for loving me. I will follow you.

Flowers and shrubs, birds and bees
in the garden that's home to Adam and Eve.

Thank you, God, for loving me. I will follow you.

Animals walk beside flowers and shrubs, birds and bees in the garden that's home to Adam and Eve.

Thank you, God, for loving me. I will follow you.

A serpent slinks on the ground near the animals walking
beside flowers and shrubs, birds and bees
in the garden that's home to Adam and Eve.

Thank you, God, for loving me. I will follow you.

A tree, an off-limits tree, where the sneaky serpent slinks
on the ground near the animals walking beside flowers
and shrubs, birds and bees
in the garden that's home to Adam and Eve.

Thank you, God, for loving me. I will follow you.

An apple, shiny and sweet, hangs from the tree,
an off-limits tree,
where the sneaky serpent slinks on the ground
near the animals walking beside flowers and shrubs, birds
and bees
in the garden that's home to Adam and Eve.

Thank you, God, for loving me. I will follow you.

A woman sees the apple, shiny and sweet,
that hangs from the tree, an off-limits tree,
where the sneaky serpent slinks on the ground
near the animals walking beside flowers and shrubs,
birds and bees
in the garden that's home to Adam and Eve.

Thank you, God, for loving me. I will follow you.

A lie told to the woman who sees the apple, shiny and sweet, that hangs from the tree, an off-limits tree, where the sneaky serpent slinks on the ground with the animals walking beside flowers and shrubs, birds and bees in the garden that's home to Adam and Eve.

Thank you, God, for loving me. I will follow you.

A bite because of the lie told to the woman
who sees the apple, shiny and sweet,
that hangs from the tree, an off-limits tree,
where the sneaky serpent slinks on the ground
with the animals walking beside flowers and shrubs, birds
and bees
in the garden that's home to Adam and Eve.

Thank you, God, for loving me. I will follow you.

A man, called to the tree, after the bite
because of the lie told to the woman
who sees the apple, shiny and sweet, that hangs from the
tree, an off-limits tree,
where the sneaky serpent slinks on the ground near the
animals walking beside flowers and shrubs, birds and
bees
in the garden that's home to Adam and Eve.

Thank you, God, for loving me. I will follow you.

A nibble he takes when called to the tree, after the bite
because of the lie told to the woman
who sees the apple, shiny and sweet, that hangs from the
tree, an off-limits tree,
where the sneaky serpent slinks on the ground
near the animals walking around flowers and shrubs,
birds and bees
in the garden that's home to Adam and Eve.

Thank you, God, for loving me. I will follow you.

This snake, smiling with glee, as the man takes a nibble
when called to the tree, after the bite
because of the lie told to the woman who sees the apple,
shiny and sweet, that hangs from the tree, an off-limits
tree, where the sneaky serpent slinks on the ground
near the animals walking beside flowers and shrubs, birds
and bees
in the garden that's home to Adam and Eve.

Thank you, God, for loving me. I will follow you.

"Hurry and hide," the two people said,
when they saw the snake, smiling with glee,
as the man takes a nibble when called to the tree,
after the bite because of the lie told to the woman
who sees the apple, shiny and sweet, that hangs from the
tree, an off-limits tree, where the sneaky serpent slinks on
the ground near the animals walking beside flowers and
shrubs, birds and bees
in the garden that's home to Adam and Eve.

Thank you, God, for loving me. I will follow you.

"We didn't listen to God," they thought
as they shouted, "Hurry and hide,"
when they saw the snake, smiling with glee,
as the man takes a nibble when called to the tree,
after the bite because of the lie told to the woman
who sees the apple, shiny and sweet, that hangs from the
tree, an off-limits tree, where the sneaky serpent slinks on
the ground near the animals walking beside flowers and
shrubs, birds and bees
in the garden that's home to Adam and Eve.

Thank you, God, for loving me. I will follow you.

Leaving the garden, sad they were tricked!
"We didn't listen to God," they thought
as they shouted "Hurry and hide,"
when they saw the snake, smiling with glee, as the man
takes a nibble when called to the tree
after the bite because of the lie told to the woman
who sees the apple, shiny and sweet, that hangs from the
tree, an off-limits tree, where the sneaky serpent slinks on
the ground
near the animals walking beside flowers and shrubs, birds
and bees
in the garden that's home to Adam and Eve.

Thank you, God, for loving me. I will follow you.

John 14:15 If you love me keep my commands.

ABOUT THE AUTHOR

DR. KRISTIN LEHR, author of *The Squirrel Family Acorn*, lives in Indiana with her husband and three sons. Her favorite thing is to spend time with family and friends. Her guilty pleasures are shopping and watching reality TV. Kristin enjoys a wonderful career as the Director of Children's Ministry at Zionsville Presbyterian Church in Zionsville, Indiana.

The Sneaky Serpent is Kristin's sixth book and the fifth in the Heaven's Heroes Series.

ABOUT THE ILLUSTRATOR

ALICIA BERRY grew up in Westfield, Indiana, and is currently a student at Columbus College of Art and Design. Studying illustration, she works with both traditional and digital media to create her artworks. She spends her summers at Lake Cumberland in Kentucky where she enjoys houseboating and waterskiing. Alicia is unsure what the future holds for her but has high hopes for this coffee-fueled artistic journey.